What Jumps?

¿Qué salta?

by Liza Charlesworth

What Jumps?

¿Qué salta?

by Liza Charlesworth

ISBN: 978-1-338-70315-3
Illustrated by Anne Kennedy
Copyright © 2020 by Liza Charlesworth. All rights reserved.
Published by Scholastic Inc., 557 Broadway, New York, NY 10012

10 9 8 7 6 5 4 3 2 1   68   20 21 22 23 24 25 26/0

Printed in Jiaxing, China. First printing, June 2020.

A grasshopper jumps.
Wow!

El grillo salta.
¡Huy!

A frog jumps.
Wow!

La rana salta.
¡Huy!

A rabbit jumps.
Wow!

El conejo salta.
¡Huy!

A kangaroo jumps.
Wow!

El canguro salta.
¡Huy!

A dolphin jumps.
Wow!

El delfín salta.
¡Huy!

A jack-in-the-box jumps.
Wow!

El muñeco salta.
¡Huy!

I jump.
Wow!

Yo salto.
¡Huy!

English-Spanish
First Little Readers™

ISBN: 978-1-338-70315-3

EAN

9 781338 703153 >

SCHOLASTIC

www.scholastic.com

In My Pocket

En mi bolsillo

by Liza Charlesworth

In My Pocket
En mi bolsillo

by Liza Charlesworth

ISBN: 978-1-338-70314-6
Illustrated by Anne Kennedy
Copyright © 2020 by Liza Charlesworth. All rights reserved.
Published by Scholastic Inc., 557 Broadway, New York, NY 10012

10 9 8 7 6 5 4 3 2 1   68   20 21 22 23 24 25 26/0

Printed in Jiaxing, China. First printing, June 2020.

Do you want to see what is in my pocket?

¿Quieres ver lo que tengo en el bolsillo?

I have a special stone.

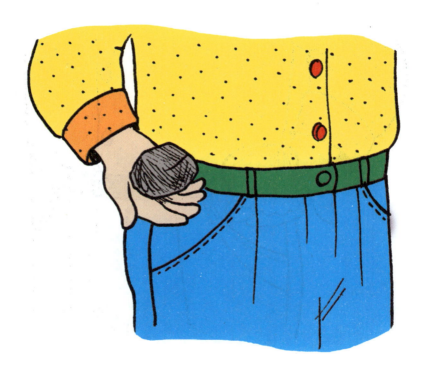

Tengo una piedra especial.

I have a special shell.

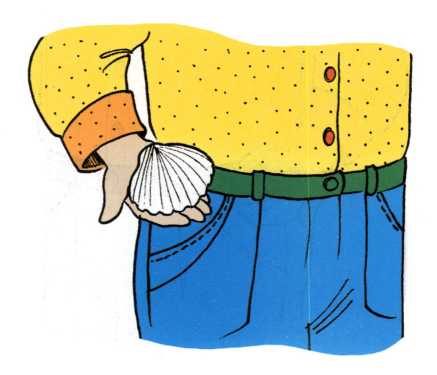

Tengo una caracola especial.

I have a special feather.

Tengo una pluma especial.

I have a special leaf.

Tengo una hoja especial.

I have a special penny.

Tengo una moneda especial.

I have a special hamster.
His name is Lenny!

Tengo un hámster especial.
¡Se llama Lenny!

English-Spanish
First Little Readers™

ISBN: 978-1-338-70314-6

EAN

9 781338 703146 >

What Do Monsters Eat?

Qué comen los monstruos?

by Liza Charlesworth

What Do Monsters Eat?
¿Qué comen los monstruos?

by Liza Charlesworth

ISBN: 978-1-338-70313-9
Illustrated by Anne Kennedy
Copyright © 2020 by Liza Charlesworth. All rights reserved.
Published by Scholastic Inc., 557 Broadway, New York, NY 10012

10 9 8 7 6 5 4 3 2 1   68   20 21 22 23 24 25 26/0

Printed in Jiaxing, China. First printing, June 2020.

Some monsters eat snakes.

Algunos monstruos
comen serpientes.

Some monsters eat cakes.

Algunos monstruos
comen pasteles.

Some monsters eat bugs.

Algunos monstruos comen insectos.

Some monsters eat rugs.

Algunos monstruos
comen alfombras.

Some monsters eat rocks.

Algunos monstruos
comen rocas.

Some monsters eat socks.

Algunos monstruos
comen medias.

What do you like to eat?

¿Qué te gusta comer a ti?

English-Spanish
First Little Readers™

ISBN: 978-1-338-70313-9

EAN

9 781338 703139

SCHOLASTIC

www.scholastic.com

Animal Crackers

Galletitas de animales

by Liza Charlesworth

Animal Crackers
Galletitas de animales

by Liza Charlesworth

ISBN: 978-1-338-70312-2
Illustrated by Anne Kennedy
Copyright © 2020 by Liza Charlesworth. All rights reserved.
Published by Scholastic Inc., 557 Broadway, New York, NY 10012

10 9 8 7 6 5 4 3 2 1   68   20 21 22 23 24 25 26/0

Printed in Jiaxing, China. First printing, June 2020.

Want to look at my animals?

¿Quieres ver mis animales?

Look at my deer.

Mira mi venado.

Look at my bear.

Mira mi oso.

Look at my ape.

Mira mi simio.

Look at my snake.

Mira mi serpiente.

Look at my cow.

Mira mi vaca.

Crunch, crunch, crunch, crunch!
Look, I have no animals now!

¡Cronch, cronch, cronch, cronch!
Mira, ¡ahora ya
no tengo animales!

English-Spanish
First Little Readers™

SCHOLASTIC

www.scholastic.com

ISBN: 978-1-338-70312-2

EAN

9 781338 703122

Farm Twins

os gemelos de la granja

by Liza Charlesworth

Farm Twins
Los gemelos de la granja

by Liza Charlesworth

ISBN: 978-1-338-70311-5
Illustrated by Anne Kennedy
Copyright © 2020 by Liza Charlesworth. All rights reserved.
Published by Scholastic Inc., 557 Broadway, New York, NY 10012

10 9 8 7 6 5 4 3 2 1   68   20 21 22 23 24 25 26/0

Printed in Jiaxing, China. First printing, June 2020.

Twin cows say, "MOO, MOO!"

Las vacas gemelas dicen:
—¡Muu, muu!

Twin pigs say, "OINK, OINK!"

Los cerdos gemelos dicen:
—¡Ruf, ruf!

Twin lambs say, "BAAH, BAAH!"

Los corderos gemelos dicen:
—¡Bee, bee!

Twin ducks say, "QUACK, QUACK!"

Los patos gemelos dicen:
—¡Cuac, cuac!

Twin chicks say, "**PEEP, PEEP!**"

Los pollitos gemelos dicen:
—¡Pío, pío!

Twin horses say, "NEIGH, NEIGH!"

Los caballos gemelos dicen:
—¡Nee, nee!

Twin girls say, "HELLO, HELLO!"

Las hermanas gemelas dicen:
—¡Hola, hola!

English-Spanish
First Little Readers™

ISBN: 978-1-338-70311-

EAN

9 781338 703115 >

The Missing Monster

El monstruo desaparecido

by Liza Charlesworth

The Missing Monster
El monstruo desaparecido

by Liza Charlesworth

ISBN: 978-1-338-70310-8
Illustrated by Anne Kennedy
Copyright © 2020 by Liza Charlesworth. All rights reserved.
Published by Scholastic Inc., 557 Broadway, New York, NY 10012

10 9 8 7 6 5 4 3 2 1   68   20 21 22 23 24 25 26/0

Printed in Jiaxing, China. First printing, June 2020.

The monster is in the box.

El monstruo está dentro
de la caja.

The monster is on the box.

El monstruo está sobre la caja.

The monster is beside the box.

El monstruo está al lado
de la caja.

The monster is over the box.

El monstruo está por encima
de la caja.

Where did the monster go?

¿Adónde se fue el monstruo?

Oh!

¡Ah!

The monster is under the box.

El monstruo está debajo
de la caja.

English-Spanish
First Little Readers™

ISBN: 978-1-338-70310-

www.scholastic.com

My Meatball

Mi albóndiga

by Liza Charlesworth

My Meatball

Mi albóndiga

by Liza Charlesworth

ISBN: 978-1-338-70309-2
Illustrated by Anne Kennedy
Copyright © 2020 by Liza Charlesworth. All rights reserved.
Published by Scholastic Inc., 557 Broadway, New York, NY 10012

10 9 8 7 6 5 4 3 2 1   68   20 21 22 23 24 25 26/0

Printed in Jiaxing, China. First printing, June 2020.

Oh, no!
My meatball rolled off my plate

¡Ay, no!
Mi albóndiga se fue rodando
del plato.

Oh, no!
It rolled past my car.

¡Ay, no!
Pasó cerca de mi carro.

Oh, no!
It rolled past my book.

¡Ay, no!
Pasó cerca de mi libro.

Oh, no!
It rolled past my blocks.

¡Ay, no!
Pasó cerca de mis bloques.

Oh, no!
It rolled past my bear.

¡Ay, no!
Pasó cerca de mi osito.

Oh, no!
It rolled past my cat.

¡Ay, no!
Pasó cerca de mi gato.

Oh, no!
No more meatball.

¡Ay, no!
Adiós, albóndiga.

English-Spanish
First Little Readers™

ISBN: 978-1-338-70309-

EAN

9 781338 703092 >

SCHOLASTIC

www.scholastic.com

Growing Up
Al crecer

by Liza Charlesworth

Growing Up
Al crecer

by Liza Charlesworth

ISBN: 978-1-338-70308-5
Illustrated by Anne Kennedy
Copyright © 2020 by Liza Charlesworth. All rights reserved.
Published by Scholastic Inc., 557 Broadway, New York, NY 10012

10 9 8 7 6 5 4 3 2 1   68   20 21 22 23 24 25 26/0

Printed in Jiaxing, China. First printing, June 2020.

A kitten grows into a cat.

Cuando crezca,
el gatito será gato.

A tadpole grows into a frog.

Cuando crezca,
el renacuajo será rana.

A lamb grows into a sheep.

Cuando crezca,
el cordero será oveja.

A puppy grows into a dog.

Cuando crezca,
el cachorro será perro.

A cub grows into a bear.

Cuando crezca,
el osezno será oso.

A piglet grows into a pig.

Cuando crezca,
el lechón será cerdo.

I will grow into a man
when I get very big!

Cuando yo crezca,
¡seré un hombre muy grande!

English-Spanish
First Little Readers™

ISBN: 978-1-338-70308-

EAN

9 781338 703085

I Wish
I Were a Bird

Quisiera ser un pájaro

by Liza Charlesworth

I Wish I Were a Bird
Quisiera ser un pájaro

by Liza Charlesworth

ISBN: 978-1-338-70316-0
Illustrated by Anne Kennedy
Copyright © 2020 by Liza Charlesworth. All rights reserved.
Published by Scholastic Inc., 557 Broadway, New York, NY 10012

10 9 8 7 6 5 4 3 2 1   68   20 21 22 23 24 25 26/0

Printed in Jiaxing, China. First printing, June 2020.

I wish I were a bird.

Quisiera ser un pájaro.

I could hatch from an egg.

Podría salir de un huevo.

I could live in a nest.

Podría vivir en un nido.

I could fly all around.

Podría volar por todas partes.

I could eat a worm.

Podría comer lombrices.

Yuck!

¡Puaj!

I wish I were a cat.

Quisiera ser un gato.

English-Spanish
First Little Readers™

ISBN: 978-1-338-70316-

EAN

9 781338 703160 >

Tiny Things

Cosas diminutas

by Liza Charlesworth

Tiny Things
Cosas diminutas

by Liza Charlesworth

ISBN: 978-1-338-70317-7
Illustrated by Anne Kennedy
Copyright © 2020 by Liza Charlesworth. All rights reserved.
Published by Scholastic Inc., 557 Broadway, New York, NY 10012

10 9 8 7 6 5 4 3 2 1   68   20 21 22 23 24 25 26/0

Printed in Jiaxing, China. First printing, June 2020.

Look in the garden.
What do you see?

Mira en el jardín.
¿Qué ves?

There is a tiny fly.

Hay una mosca diminuta.

There is a tiny ladybug.

Hay una mariquita diminuta.

There is a tiny grasshopper.

Hay un saltamontes diminuto.

There is a tiny bee.

Hay una abeja diminuta.

There is a tiny ant.

Hay una hormiga diminuta.

There is a giant me!

Hay una gigante. ¡Soy yo!

English-Spanish
First Little Readers™

ISBN: 978-1-338-70317-

SCHOLASTIC

www.scholastic.com

EAN

9 781338 703177 >

Gingerbread Boy
El muñeco de pan de jengibre

by Liza Charlesworth

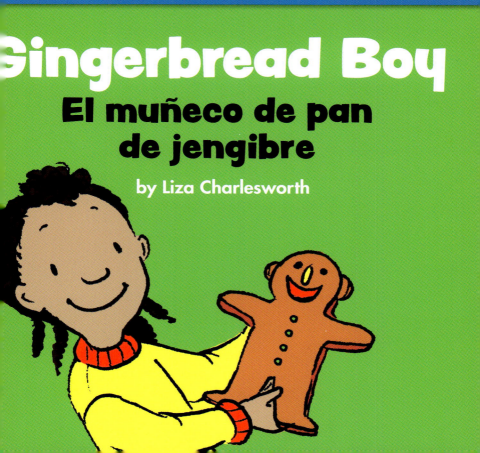

Gingerbread Boy
El muñeco de pan de jengibre

by Liza Charlesworth

ISBN: 978-1-338-70307-8
Illustrated by Anne Kennedy
Copyright © 2020 by Liza Charlesworth. All rights reserved.
Published by Scholastic Inc., 557 Broadway, New York, NY 10012

10 9 8 7 6 5 4 3 2 1   68   20 21 22 23 24 25 26/0

Printed in Jiaxing, China. First printing, June 2020.

SCHOLASTIC

Let's make a gingerbread boy.

Vamos a hacer
un muñeco de pan de jengibre.

First, I put on two eyes.

Primero, le pongo los dos ojos.

Then, I put on one nose.

Después, le pongo una nariz.

Then, I put on one mouth.

Después, le pongo una boca.

Then, I put on four buttons.

Después, le pongo cuatro botones

Then, I put on two ears.

Después, le pongo dos orejas.

Hey! Come back here!

¡Oye! ¡Ven acá!

English-Spanish
First Little Readers™

SCHOLASTIC

www.scholastic.com

ISBN: 978-1-338-70307-

EAN

9 781338 703078 >

What Flies?

¿Qué vuela?

by Liza Charlesworth

What Flies?

¿Qué vuela?

by Liza Charlesworth

ISBN: 978-1-338-70306-1
Illustrated by Anne Kennedy
Copyright © 2020 by Liza Charlesworth. All rights reserved.
Published by Scholastic Inc., 557 Broadway, New York, NY 10012

10 9 8 7 6 5 4 3 2 1   68   20 21 22 23 24 25 26/0

Printed in Jiaxing, China. First printing, June 2020.

What flies in the sky?

¿Qué vuela en el cielo?

A bee flies way up high!

¡La abeja vuela muy alto!

A bird flies way up high!

¡El pájaro vuela muy alto!

A kite flies way up high!

¡La cometa vuela muy alto!

A plane flies way up high!

¡El avión vuela muy alto!

I fly way up high...

Yo vuelo muy alto...

but only in my dreams!

¡pero solo en sueños!

English-Spanish
First Little Readers™

SCHOLASTIC

www.scholastic.com

ISBN: 978-1-338-70306-

EAN

Bigger
Más grande

by Liza Charlesworth

Bigger
Más grande

by Liza Charlesworth

ISBN: 978-1-338-70305-4
Illustrated by Anne Kennedy
Copyright © 2020 by Liza Charlesworth. All rights reserved.
Published by Scholastic Inc., 557 Broadway, New York, NY 10012

10 9 8 7 6 5 4 3 2 1   68   20 21 22 23 24 25 26/0

Printed in Jiaxing, China. First printing, June 2020.

The cat is bigger than
the mouse.

El gato es más grande que
el ratón.

The dog is bigger than
the cat.

El perro es más grande que
el gato.

The gorilla is bigger than
the dog.

El gorila es más grande que
el perro.

The bear is bigger than
the gorilla.

El oso es más grande que
el gorila.

The rhino is bigger than
the bear.

El rinoceronte es más grande que
el oso.

The elephant is bigger than
the rhino.

El elefante es más grande que
el rinoceronte.

But guess what?
The big elephant is
afraid of the little mouse!

Pero, ¿sabes qué?
¡El elefante grande le tiene
miedo al ratón pequeño!

English-Spanish

First Little Readers™

ISBN: 978-1-338-70305-

EAN

9 781338 703054

I Like Socks
Me gustan las medias

by Liza Charlesworth

I Like Socks
Me gustan las medias

by Liza Charlesworth

ISBN: 978-1-338-70304-7
Illustrated by Anne Kennedy
Copyright © 2020 by Liza Charlesworth. All rights reserved.
Published by Scholastic Inc., 557 Broadway, New York, NY 10012

10 9 8 7 6 5 4 3 2 1   68   20 21 22 23 24 25 26/0

Printed in Jiaxing, China. First printing, June 2020.

I like socks with lots of cars!

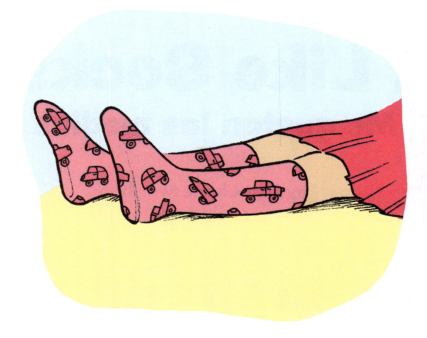

¡Me gustan las medias
con muchos autos!

I like socks with lots of stars!

¡Me gustan las medias
con muchas estrellas!

I like socks with lots of bells!

¡Me gustan las medias
con muchas campanas!

I like socks with lots of shells!

¡Me gustan las medias
con muchas caracolas!

I like socks with lots of dice!

¡Me gustan las medias
con muchos dados!

I like socks with lots of mice...

Me gustan las medias
con muchos ratones...

and so does my cat!

¡y a mi gato también!

English-Spanish
First Little Readers™

SCHOLASTIC

www.scholastic.com

ISBN: 978-1-338-70304

EAN

9 781338 703047

Meet My Baby Brother

e presento a mi hermanito

by Liza Charlesworth

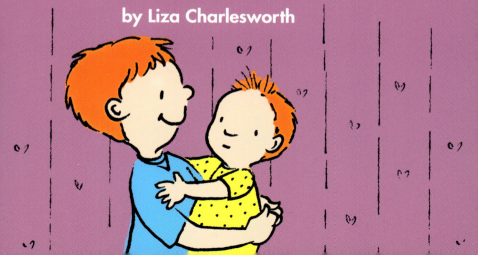

Meet My Baby Brother

Te presento a mi hermanito

by Liza Charlesworth

ISBN: 978-1-338-70303-0
Illustrated by Anne Kennedy
Copyright © 2020 by Liza Charlesworth. All rights reserved.
Published by Scholastic Inc., 557 Broadway, New York, NY 10012

10 9 8 7 6 5 4 3 2 1   68   20 21 22 23 24 25 26/0

Printed in Jiaxing, China. First printing, June 2020.

Here is my baby brother.
His name is Ray.

Te presento a mi hermanito.
Se llama Ray.

He likes to crawl and crawl.

Le gusta gatear y gatear.

He likes to play and play.

Le gusta jugar y jugar.

He likes to cry and cry.

Le gusta llorar y llorar.

He likes to sleep and sleep.

Le gusta dormir y dormir.

He likes to eat and eat!

¡Le gusta comer y comer!

It's just too bad
he is not so neat!

¡Es una pena que
no sea muy limpio!

English-Spanish
First Little Readers™

ISBN: 978-1-338-70303-0

EAN

9 781338 703030 >

SCHOLASTIC

www.scholastic.com

Come Over

Ven a verme

by Liza Charlesworth

Come Over
Ven a verme

by Liza Charlesworth

ISBN: 978-1-338-70302-3
Illustrated by Anne Kennedy
Copyright © 2020 by Liza Charlesworth. All rights reserved.
Published by Scholastic Inc., 557 Broadway, New York, NY 10012

10 9 8 7 6 5 4 3 2 1   68   20 21 22 23 24 25 26/0

Printed in Jiaxing, China. First printing, June 2020.

Come over and see my chair.

Ven a ver mi silla.

Come over and see my table.

Ven a ver mi mesa.

Come over and see my lamp.

Ven a ver mi lámpara.

Come over and see my tub.

Ven a ver mi bañera.

Come over and see my couch

Ven a ver mi sofá.

Come over and see my dresser.

Ven a ver mi cómoda.

Come over and see
my dollhouse!

¡Ven a ver
mi casa de muñecas!

English-Spanish

First Little Readers™

ISBN: 978-1-338-70302-

EAN

9 781338 703023 >

SCHOLASTIC

www.scholastic.com

Party Shapes

as figuras de la fiesta

by Liza Charlesworth

Party Shapes
Las figuras de la fiesta

by Liza Charlesworth

ISBN: 978-1-338-70301-6
Illustrated by Anne Kennedy
Copyright © 2020 by Liza Charlesworth. All rights reserved.
Published by Scholastic Inc., 557 Broadway, New York, NY 10012

10 9 8 7 6 5 4 3 2 1   68   20 21 22 23 24 25 26/0

Printed in Jiaxing, China. First printing, June 2020.

Come to my party
and see the shapes.

Ven a mi fiesta
a ver las figuras.

Here is a hat.
It is a triangle.

Aquí está el sombrero.
Es un triángulo.

Here is a game.
It is a rectangle.

Aquí está el juego.
Es un rectángulo.

Here is a present.
It is a square.

Aquí está el regalo.
Es un cuadrado.

Here is a birthday cake.
It is a circle.

Aquí está el pastel de cumpleaños.
Es un círculo.

Here is a balloon.
It is an oval.

Aquí está el globo.
Es un óvalo.

POP!
It was an oval.

¡POP!
Era un óvalo.

English-Spanish
First Little Readers™

ISBN: 978-1-338-70301

EAN

9 781338 703016 >

SCHOLASTIC

www.scholastic.com

The Wheels on the Bus
Las ruedas del autobús

by Liza Charlesworth

The Wheels on the Bus
Las ruedas del autobús

by Liza Charlesworth

ISBN: 978-1-338-70299-6
Illustrated by Anne Kennedy
Copyright © 2020 by Liza Charlesworth. All rights reserved.
Published by Scholastic Inc., 557 Broadway, New York, NY 10012

10 9 8 7 6 5 4 3 2 1   68   20 21 22 23 24 25 26/0

Printed in Jiaxing, China. First printing, June 2020.

The wheels on the bus
go round and round.

Las ruedas del autobús
dan vueltas y vueltas.

The wheels on the car
go round and round.

Las ruedas del auto
dan vueltas y vueltas.

3

The wheels on the van
go round and round.

Las ruedas de la camioneta
dan vueltas y vueltas.

The wheels on the motorcycle
go round and round.

Las ruedas de la motocicleta
dan vueltas y vueltas.

The wheels on the truck
go round and round.

Las ruedas del camión
dan vueltas y vueltas.

The wheels on the fire engine
go round and round.

Las ruedas del camión
de bomberos
dan vueltas y vueltas.

The wheels on the vehicles
go round and round,
all through my room!

Las ruedas de los vehículos
dan vueltas y vueltas,
¡por toda mi habitación!

English-Spanish
First Little Readers™

ISBN: 978-1-338-70299-
EAN
9 781338 702996 >

www.scholastic.com

Cloud Pictures

Nubes con formas

by Liza Charlesworth

Cloud Pictures
Nubes con formas

by Liza Charlesworth

ISBN: 978-1-338-70297-2
Illustrated by Anne Kennedy
Copyright © 2020 by Liza Charlesworth. All rights reserved.
Published by Scholastic Inc., 557 Broadway, New York, NY 10012

10 9 8 7 6 5 4 3 2 1   68   20 21 22 23 24 25 26/0

Printed in Jiaxing, China. First printing, June 2020.

I like to look up in the sky and see the pictures floating by.

Me gusta mirar al cielo
y ver pasar las nubes
de diferentes formas.

Look! I see a cloud hat.

¡Mira!
Esta nube es un sombrero.

Look! I see a cloud bat.

¡Mira!
Esta nube es un murciélago.

Look! I see a cloud flower.

¡Mira!
Esta nube es una flor.

Look! I see a cloud tower.

¡Mira!
Esta nube es una torre.

Look! I see a cloud tree.

¡Mira!
Esta nube es un árbol.

Look! I see a cloud me!

¡Mira!
¡Esta nube soy yo!

English-Spanish
First Little Readers™

SCHOLASTIC

www.scholastic.com

ISBN: 978-1-338-70297-

EAN

9 781338 702972 >

Ice Cream Scoops

Bolas de helado

by Liza Charlesworth

Ice Cream Scoops

Bolas de helado

by Liza Charlesworth

ISBN: 978-1-338-70298-9
Illustrated by Anne Kennedy
Copyright © 2020 by Liza Charlesworth. All rights reserved.
Published by Scholastic Inc., 557 Broadway, New York, NY 10012

10 9 8 7 6 5 4 3 2 1   68   20 21 22 23 24 25 26/0

Printed in Jiaxing, China. First printing, June 2020.

This cone has one scoop
of ice cream.
May I have more, please?

Este barquillo tiene
una bola de helado.
¿Me sirves más, por favor?

This cone has two scoops
of ice cream.
May I have more, please?

Este barquillo tiene
dos bolas de helado.
¿Me sirves más, por favor?

This cone has three scoops
of ice cream.
May I have more, please?

Este barquillo tiene tres bolas
de helado.
¿Me sirves más, por favor?

This cone has four scoops
of ice cream.
May I have more, please?

Este barquillo tiene cuatro bolas
de helado.
¿Me sirves más, por favor?

This cone has five scoops
of ice cream.
May I have more, please?

Este barquillo tiene cinco bolas
de helado.
¿Me sirves más, por favor?

Oh, no!

¡Ay, no!

This cone has no scoops
of ice cream.
May I have more, please?

Este barquillo no tiene bolas
de helado.
¿Me sirves más, por favor?

English-Spanish
First Little Readers™

ISBN: 978-1-338-70298-

EAN

9 781338 702989 >

SCHOLASTIC

www.scholastic.com

Clean Up, Clean Up!

¡A recoger, a recoger!

by Liza Charlesworth

Clean Up, Clean Up!

¡A recoger, a recoger!

by Liza Charlesworth

ISBN: 978-1-338-70318-4
Illustrated by Anne Kennedy
Copyright © 2020 by Liza Charlesworth. All rights reserved.
Published by Scholastic Inc., 557 Broadway, New York, NY 10012

10 9 8 7 6 5 4 3 2 1   68   20 21 22 23 24 25 26/0

Printed in Jiaxing, China. First printing, June 2020.

Clean up, clean up!
I put my crayons in the box.

¡A recoger, a recoger!
Pongo mis crayones en la caja.

Clean up, clean up!
I put my books on the shelf.

¡A recoger, a recoger!
Pongo mis libros en el estante.

Clean up, clean up!
I put my clothes in the drawer.

¡A recoger, a recoger!
Pongo mi ropa en el cajón.

Clean up, clean up!
I put my shoes in the closet.

¡A recoger, a recoger!
Pongo mis zapatos en el armario.

Clean up, clean up!
I put my trash in the can.

¡A recoger, a recoger!
Pongo mi basura en el cesto.

Clean up, clean up!
I put my bear on the bed.

¡A recoger, a recoger!
Pongo mi osito en la cama.

"Good work, good work!"
Daddy said.

—¡Bien hecho, bien hecho!
—dijo mi papá.

English-Spanish
First Little Readers™

ISBN: 978-1-338-70318-

EAN

9 781338 703184 >

SCHOLASTIC

www.scholastic.com

Great Hair
Cabellos hermosos

by Liza Charlesworth

Great Hair
Cabellos hermosos

by Liza Charlesworth

ISBN: 978-1-338-70319-1
Illustrated by Anne Kennedy
Copyright © 2020 by Liza Charlesworth. All rights reserved.
Published by Scholastic Inc., 557 Broadway, New York, NY 10012

10 9 8 7 6 5 4 3 2 1   68   20 21 22 23 24 25 26/0

Printed in Jiaxing, China. First printing, June 2020.

She has long hair.

Ella tiene el cabello largo.

He has short hair.

Él tiene el cabello corto.

She has dark hair.

Ella tiene el cabello oscuro.

He has light hair.

Él tiene el cabello claro.

She has curly hair.

Ella tiene el cabello rizado.

He has straight hair.

Él tiene el cabello lacio.

But all these kids
have really great hair!

¡Todos tienen
cabellos hermosos!

English-Spanish
First Little Readers™

ISBN: 978-1-338-70319-

EAN

9 781338 703191 >

SCHOLASTIC

www.scholastic.com

Halloween

Halloween

by Liza Charlesworth

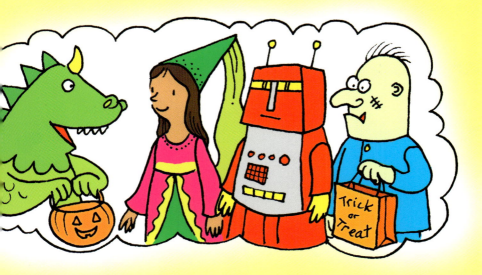

Halloween

Halloween

by Liza Charlesworth

ISBN: 978-1-338-70320-7
Illustrated by Anne Kennedy
Copyright © 2020 by Liza Charlesworth. All rights reserved.
Published by Scholastic Inc., 557 Broadway, New York, NY 10012

10 9 8 7 6 5 4 3 2 1   68   20 21 22 23 24 25 26/0

Printed in Jiaxing, China. First printing, June 2020.

Here is a dragon.

Aquí está el dragón.

Here is an astronaut.

Aquí está el astronauta.

Here is a monster.

Aquí está el monstruo.

Here is a princess.

Aquí está la princesa.

Here is a robot.

Aquí está el robot.

Here is a tiger.

Aquí está el tigre.

No, it is just us!
Happy Halloween!

¡No, somos solo nosotros!
¡Feliz Fiesta de Halloween!

English-Spanish
First Little Readers™

ISBN: 978-1-338-70320-

EAN

9 781338 703207 >

www.scholastic.com

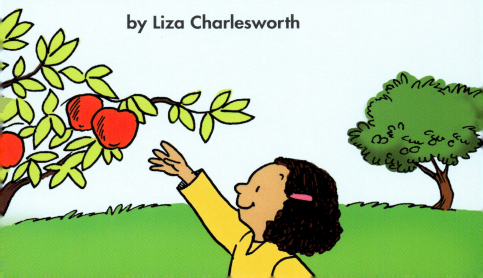

What Grows on Trees?

Qué crece en los árboles?

by Liza Charlesworth

What Grows on Trees?
¿Qué crece en los árboles?

by Liza Charlesworth

ISBN: 978-1-338-70321-4
Illustrated by Anne Kennedy
Copyright © 2020 by Liza Charlesworth. All rights reserved.
Published by Scholastic Inc., 557 Broadway, New York, NY 10012

10 9 8 7 6 5 4 3 2 1   68   20 21 22 23 24 25 26/0

Printed in Jiaxing, China. First printing, June 2020.

Do apples grow on trees?
Yes!

¿Crecen las manzanas
en los árboles?
¡Sí!

Do cherries grow on trees?
Yes!

¿Crecen las cerezas
en los árboles?
¡Sí!

Do peaches grow on trees?
Yes!

¿Crecen los melocotones
en los árboles?
¡Sí!

Do pears grow on trees?
Yes!

¿Crecen las peras
en los árboles?
¡Sí!

Do oranges grow on trees?
Yes!

¿Crecen las naranjas
en los árboles?
¡Sí!

Do bananas grow on trees?
Yes!

¿Crecen los plátanos
en los árboles?
¡Sí!

Do cupcakes grow on trees?
No! But if they did,
I would be pleased.

¿Crecen las magdalenas
en los árboles?
¡No! Pero si lo hicieran,
sería fantástico.

English-Spanish
First Little Readers™

ISBN: 978-1-338-70321-4

EAN

9 781338 703214 >

SCHOLASTIC

www.scholastic.com

Draw a Cat

Dibuja un gato

by Liza Charlesworth

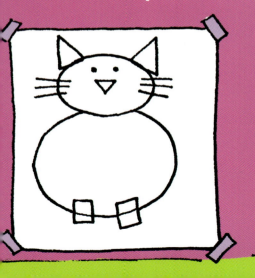

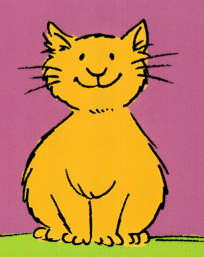

Draw a Cat
Dibuja un gato

by Liza Charlesworth

ISBN: 978-1-338-70322-1
Illustrated by Anne Kennedy
Copyright © 2020 by Liza Charlesworth. All rights reserved.
Published by Scholastic Inc., 557 Broadway, New York, NY 10012

10 9 8 7 6 5 4 3 2 1   68   20 21 22 23 24 25 26/0

Printed in Jiaxing, China. First printing, June 2020.

SCHOLASTIC

Want to see me draw a cat?

¿Quieres verme dibujar un gato?

I draw 2 circles.
Just like that!

Dibujo 2 círculos.
¡Así!

I draw 2 squares.
Just like that!

Dibujo 2 cuadrados.
¡Así!

I draw 3 triangles.
Just like that!

Dibujo 3 triángulos.
¡Así!

I draw **2** dots.
Just like that!

Dibujo **2** puntos.
¡Así!

I draw 6 lines.
Just like that!

Dibujo 6 líneas.
¡Así!

I drew a cat.
Just like that!
Now, you try!

Dibujé un gato.
¡Así!
Ahora, ¡inténtalo!

English-Spanish

First Little Readers™

ISBN: 978-1-338-70322-1

EAN

9 781338 703221